TRIVIA
QUIZ BOOK

Other Teenage Mutant Ninja Turtles® books available in Yearling Books:

Teenage Mutant Ninja Turtles®
  (a novelization of the movie) by B. B. Hiller
Teenage Mutant Ninja Turtles® II The Secret of the Ooze™
  (a novelization of the movie) by B. B. Hiller
Buried Treasure by Dave Morris
Sky High by Dave Morris
Red Herrings by Dave Morris
Six-Guns and Shurikens by Dave Morris
Dinosaur Farm by Dave Morris
Splinter to the Fore by Dave Morris

YEARLING BOOKS/YOUNG YEARLINGS/YEARLING CLASSICS are designed especially to entertain and enlighten young people. Patricia Reilly Giff, consultant to this series, received her bachelor's degree from Marymount College and a master's degree in history from St. John's University. She holds a Professional Diploma in Reading and a Doctorate of Humane Letters from Hofstra University. She was a teacher and reading consultant for many years, and is the author of numerous books for young readers.

For a complete listing of all Yearling titles, write to
Dell Readers Service
P.O. Box 1045
South Holland, IL 60473.

TRIVIA
QUIZ BOOK

MICHAEL LANDER

ILLUSTRATED BY FRANCIS MAO

A YEARLING BOOK

Published by
Dell Publishing
a division of
Bantam Doubleday Dell Publishing Group, Inc.
666 Fifth Avenue
New York, New York 10103

ISBN: 0-440-40543-2

Printed in the United States of America

July 1991

10 9 8 7 6 5 4 3 2 1

For my parents
and
For my friends at MWS, who provided me
with one of my most interesting experiences
in animation.

Special Thanks to
A.C.W. and David Gale at Dell for making
this book happen.

CONTENTS

PART ONE
Trivia Questions

1

◆◆◆◆◆◆◆◆◆◆◆◆◆◆◆◆◆◆◆◆◆◆◆◆◆

TMNT® CARTOON TRIVIA QUESTIONS
page 3

2

▼▼▼▼▼▼▼▼▼▼▼▼▼▼▼▼▼▼▼▼▼▼▼▼▼▼

TMNT® MOVIE TRIVIA QUESTIONS
page 14

3

●●●●●●●●●●●●●●●●●●●●●●●●●●●

TMNT® II: *THE SECRET OF THE OOZE*™ MOVIE TRIVIA QUESTIONS
page 24

4

■ ■

ARCHIE® COMIC BOOK SERIES: TMNT® ADVENTURES TRIVIA QUESTIONS
page 32

5

★ ★

PLAYMATES® TOYS: TMNT® TRIVIA QUESTIONS
page 37

PART TWO
Trivia Question Answers

1

◆ ◆

TMNT® CARTOON TRIVIA ANSWERS
page 43

2

▼ ▼

TMNT® MOVIE TRIVIA ANSWERS
page 52

3

• •

TMNT® II: *THE SECRET OF THE OOZE*™ MOVIE TRIVIA ANSWERS

page 58

4

■ ■

ARCHIE® COMIC BOOK SERIES: TMNT® ADVENTURES TRIVIA ANSWERS

page 63

5

★ ★

PLAYMATES® TOYS: TMNT® TRIVIA ANSWERS

page 67

PART ONE

TRIVIA
QUESTIONS

TMNT® CARTOON TRIVIA QUESTIONS

(Answers to Section One begin on page 43.)

A. Simple Level Questions:

1. Name the four Teenage Mutant Ninja Turtles®.

2. Who were they named after?

3. What is the Turtles' motto?

4. Who is Splinter?

5. What mutant animal is Splinter?

6. Where do the Turtles live?

7. What is the Turtles' favorite food?

8. What weapon does Leonardo use?

9. What weapon does Michaelangelo use?

10. What weapon does Raphael use?

11. What weapon does Donatello use?

12. Who is April O'Neil?

13. At what news station does she work?

14. What does April carry with her at all times?

15. Who is April's boss?

16. Who is April's rival reporter?

17. Who is Irma?

18. Who are the Turtles' arch enemies?

19. Who are Shredder's evil sidekicks?

20. What mutant animals are they?

21. Shredder is the leader of what clan?

22. Who are Shredder's faithful followers?

23. What are the Foot Soldiers?

24. What marking is imprinted on their face masks?

25. What weapon do the Foot Soldiers carry?

26. Who is Krang?

27. How does Krang get around?

28. Where is Krang from?

29. How does he get to Earth from there?

30. What is the name of Shredder's headquarters?

31. Where is it hidden?

32. How do Shredder, Bebop, and Rocksteady travel?

33. Who is General Tragg?

34. Who are his followers?

35. How do the Turtles keep in touch with April?

36. What does it look like?

37. How do the Turtles get around the city streets?

38. What do the Turtles use to fly over the city?

39. What detaches from it?

40. What is the cheapskate?

41. What is Michaelangelo's favorite saying?

B. Medium Level Questions:

42. What is the art of self-defense practiced by the Turtles?

43. What name do the Turtles call Shredder?

44. What name do Rocksteady and Bebop call the Turtles?

45. Who is the evil mutant alligator?

46. What are his favorite sayings?

47. Who is Casey Jones?

48. What weapon does Casey carry?

49. Who is the Rat King?

50. Who are the Punk Frogs?

51. Where are they from?

52. What do the Turtles wear when they go undercover?

53. Which Turtle is the leader?

54. Which Turtle is the scientific inventor?

55. Who is Baxter Stockman?

56. What was he before being transformed?

57. Who is Metalhead?

58. Who is known as "New York's Shiniest"?

59. What is the "Knucklehead"?

60. What is the "Turtle Terminator"?

61. How does the "Turtle Terminator" function?

C. "Stumpers" Questions:

62. What female ninja was a threat to the Turtles?

63. What did she leave behind at the scene of the crime as her calling card?

64. What is Shredder's original name?

65. What is Splinter's original name?

66. What street is the Channel 6 building located on?

67. What sculpture is in the main lobby of the Channel 6 building?

68. What Princess was April once mistaken for?

69. What is the name of the Turtles' favorite pizza parlor?

70. What job did Michaelangelo once take in order to earn extra money?

71. What mutant/animal did April once turn into?

72. What is Burne Thompson's girlfriend's name?

73. What is the name of April's television program?

74. What are the names of the Punk Frogs?

75. Who were the Punk Frogs named after?

76. What are the Punk Frogs' weapons?

77. Who are the Turtles' teenage friends from Dimension X?

78. What are their names?

79. Which Turtle has a crush on Kala, the Nutrino?

80. What do the Nutrinos drive around in?

81. What is the Grybyx?

82. Whose pet is the Grybyx?

83. What is the Grybyx's special power?

84. What happens if you feed a Grybyx Earth food?

85. What is the antidote?

86. What hero is the Turtles' rabbit friend?

87. What powers does he have?

88. What human detective friend solved the case of the "Hot Kimono"?

89. Who was the leader of a gang April once joined undercover?

90. What magician friend of the Turtles' causes all sorts of problems?

91. What human boy is known as the "Fifth Turtle"?

92. How does he always find the Turtles?

93. How does Zach save the Turtles and himself from Shredder?

94. In the episode "Beware the Lotus," what does Krang offer Lotus to destroy the Turtles?

95. Which Turtle has a crush on Lotus?

96. In the episode "Enter the Rat King," why does the Rat King kidnap April?

97. How does the Rat King control his rats?

98. What is the Rat King's evil plot?

99. What was the Big MACC?

100. Who is Mr. Ogg?

101. What is the name of "New York's Shiniest"?

102. What does it stand for?

103. What is "The Eye of Sarnath"?

104. In the episode "It Came from Beneath the Sewers," a piece of "The Eye of Sarnath" turns what object into a monster?

105. In the episode "Mean Machine," what is the name of the evil computer created by "The Eye of Sarnath"?

106. When Shredder pieces together "The Eye of Sarnath," what does he do with it?

107. Who finds the helmet by accident?

108. In the episode "Enter the Fly," with what does Shredder try to poison April?

109. What is the antidote?

110. What device does Krang give Shredder to transfer energy to a portal opening in order to get the Technodrome to Earth?

111. What does Krang tap into for the energy needed to open the portal?

112. In the episode "Attack of the Killer Pizzas," what is the danger?

113. In the episode "Attack of the Killer Pizzas," how did these creatures hatch?

114. Who are Rocksteady and Bebop's heroic alter egos?

115. What talk show program did the Turtles appear on?

116. How did the Turtles protect themselves when Shredder used a degravitational device on the city?

117. In "Bye, Bye, Fly," Baxter Stockman has a device that turns Michaelangelo into what animal?

118. In the episode "Corporate Raiders from Dimension X," what corporation does Shredder take over in order to rule the city's business?

119. In the episode "Corporate Raiders from Dimension X," what friend of the Turtles takes a job at this corporation and tries to stop Shredder?

120. In the episode "Turtle Terminator," how do the Turtles destroy the robot?

121. In the episode "Leatherhead—Terror of the Swamp," who does Leatherhead enslave as his prisoners?

122. After Leatherhead is captured by the Turtles, how does he trick them?

123. In that same episode, what happens to Shredder when he falls into the mutagen-tainted river?

124. In the episode "The Old Switcheroo," Shredder believes he has been turned into which Turtle?

125. In the episode "The Missing Map," on what is the map written?

126. In the episode "Attack of the Big MACC," how far into the future has this machine come from?

127. In the episode "Attack of the Big MACC," what device does Shredder use to get the Big MACC?

TMNT® MOVIE
TRIVIA QUESTIONS

(Answers to Section Two begin on page 52.)

A. Simple Level Questions:

1. In which city does the story take place?

2. Who is the newswoman reporting about crime in the city?

3. What channel does she work for?

4. Who is April's boss?

5. What is April's boss's son's name?

6. What is the name of the gang that he belongs to?

7. After rescuing April from gang members in the beginning of the story, which Turtle leaves his weapon behind at the scene of the crime?

8. What weapon is it that April finds and takes?

9. Where do the Turtles order their pizza from?

10. Which Turtle goes out to see a movie?

11. Which Turtle has a crush on April?

12. Which Turtle brings April to their sewer hideout?

13. Why does he do that?

14. Who does Raphael meet in Central Park while catching purse snatchers?

15. What does Casey wear over his face?

16. What weapon does he carry around?

17. Above what type of store does April live?

18. Who gets kidnapped by the Foot Clan?

19. Which Turtle gets beaten up badly by the Foot Clan?

20. What happens to April's apartment?

21. Where do the Turtles, April, and Casey escape to?

22. Who talks to Splinter while he is tied up by Shredder?

23. Who follows Danny back to Shredder's hideout, once they return from the country?

24. How does he disguise himself?

Which Turtle goes out to see a movie?

25. Why does Splinter hate Shredder?

26. What did Splinter do to Shredder when this happened?

27. What did Shredder do in return?

28. How is Shredder defeated?

29. Where does Shredder ultimately end?

B. Medium Level Questions:

30. At what station does April work?

31. What is the name of the antique shop she lives above?

32. Who owns the shop?

33. Which Turtle does April thank on the news?

34. How much money does Danny steal from April's purse?

35. What nonsense saying does Donatello come up with that rhymes with Chevy Nova?

36. What item do the Turtles hate on their pizza?

37. Splinter teaches the Turtles that: "The Art of Ninja is the Art of . . . ?"

38. What movie does Raphael go to see?

39. What other type of bat does Casey Jones use to beat Raphael?

40. What was Casey Jones before he became a crime fighter?

41. When the Foot Soldiers attack the Turtles at April's apartment, who gets dunked in the aquarium?

42. What type of weapon, other than the *nunchakus*, *bos*, *sais*, and swords, do the Foot Clan use?

43. What does Casey Jones use as a weapon against Shredder's right-hand man in the warehouse?

44. After Splinter defeats Shredder, he tells them that a worse fate than death is "death without . . ."

45. What is the key difference in the origin of Splinter in the movie compared to the television cartoon version?

C. "Stumpers" Questions:

46. What name is printed on the back of Danny's T-shirt in the opening of the movie?

47. Whose picture is on the front of his T-shirt?

48. What is the *New York Post* headline in the opening of the movie?

49. What does the police department refer to this criminal activity as?

50. What is the name of the Chief of Police?

51. What is printed on the side of the getaway van in the opening of the movie?

52. Splinter tells the Turtles that "their territory is the . . ."?

53. What is the name of the song the Turtles dance to in their sewer hideout after eating?

54. How late is the Dominoes Pizza delivery man?

55. Where is the cab passenger going when Raphael rolls over the cab's front?

56. What type of baseball bat does Casey Jones use against Raphael?

57. Where is April's apartment located?

58. What stuffed animal is on the floor of her apartment?

59. What are the images on her shower curtain?

60. What is the second *New York Post* headline?

61. At what subway station is April confronted by the Foot Clan?

62. What is the name of Shredder's right-hand man?

63. What type of golf club does Casey Jones defeat him with?

64. What is the Foot Soldiers' costume?

65. What is the cartoon the Turtles watch at April's apartment?

66. Which Turtle befriends Casey Jones while fixing the truck?

67. What television show do they make jokes about while fixing the truck?

68. Which Turtle wears a cowboy hat while practicing in the country?

69. What board game are the Turtles playing before they leave?

70. What phobia does Casey Jones have?

71. What is the name of Yoshi's girlfriend who Oroku Saki killed?

72. Which Turtle does Danny have a drawing of that Shredder finds?

73. What weapon does Shredder use against the Turtles and Splinter?

74. Where do the former Foot Soldiers tell the police the hideout is?

75. Which Turtle does teen movie star Corey Feldman provide the voice for?

TMNT® II:
THE SECRET OF
THE OOZE™ MOVIE
TRIVIA QUESTIONS

(Answers to Section Three begin on page 58.)

A. Simple Level Questions:

1. What food is everybody eating at the beginning of the movie?

2. Who is the young pizza delivery boy?

3. When the delivery boy is saved by the Turtles from a group of robbers, where do they put him to keep him out of danger?

4. Which Turtle uses a yo-yo as a makeshift weapon?

5. What food item does Michaelangelo use as nunchucks?

6. Where is the Turtles' temporary home?

7. What punishment does Splinter have the Turtles do for their misbehavior?

24

Where is T.G.R.I. located?

8. What is the name of the chemical company that manufactures the "ooze"?

9. Where is it located?

10. What flower was mutated by the "ooze"?

11. What mutant animals does Shredder create to battle the Turtles?

12. Where do the Turtles make their new home?

13. Which rap singer is performing at the nightclub that the Turtles and Shredder's mutants crash into?

14. How do the Turtles get Shredder out of the nightclub?

15. What happens to Shredder when he lands in the water?

16. How is Shredder finally killed?

17. What is the name of the pizza parlor Keno works for?

18. What are the three stores in the mall that are being robbed when Keno arrives?

19. What yo-yo tricks does Michaelangelo perform?

20. What toy does April find in her refrigerator?

21. Who does April's new assistant secretly work for?

22. Which Turtle helps Keno pass the Foot's test?

23. How does Shredder trap the other Turtles?

24. With what weapon does Splinter shoot down the net?

25. What is the name of the mutant snapping turtle?

26. What is the name of the mutant wolf?

27. What does the professor make the antimutagen into?

28. What do the Turtles sneak the antimutagen into in order to fool Tokka and Rahzar?

29. When the antimutagen ice cubes don't work, what do the Turtles use against Tokka and Rahzar to get them back to their former state?

30. What song does Vanilla Ice create while the Turtles are fighting?

31. Who storms into the club and tries to attack Shredder on stage?

32. How do the Turtles survive the collapse of the dock?

C. "Stumpers" Questions:

33. On what street is Roy's Pizza located?

34. Where is April's new apartment?

35. Which Turtle is first made to do back flips for misbehaving?

36. What does T.G.R.I. stand for?

37. What is the name of the professor who works for T.G.R.I.?

38. What is the name of April's assistant and Foot Clan member?

39. What is the lot number of the canister of mutagen that Shredder steals?

40. Who is the model on the poster that Michaelangelo takes off the wall as the Turtles pack to leave April's apartment?

41. What movie does Michaelangelo do an impersonation from, when he says good-bye to April?

42. What is the name of April's news manager?

43. What news story is the news manager about to assign April to?

44. How many seconds does Keno have to remove all the bells from the dummy in the Foot Clan's ninja test?

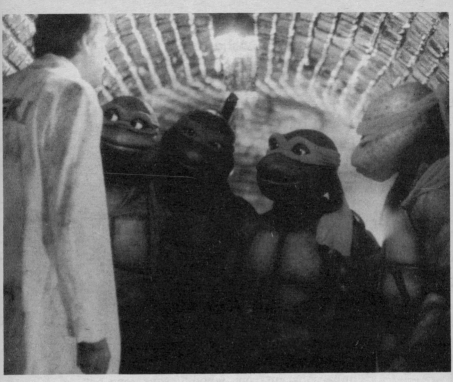

What is the name of the professor who works for T.G.R.I.?

45. What bridge does Keno run back over to alert the Turtles that Raphael has been caught?

46. What is the first word both Tokka and Rahzar say?

47. What other news van arrives on the scene after Tokka and Rahzar have destroyed a street block?

48. What precinct does Police Chief Sterns work in?

49. What temperature is the antimutagen heated at?

50. What type of glass does the professor mix the antimutagen in?

51. What is the name of the nightclub?

52. Why don't the antimutagen ice cubes work against Tokka and Rahzar?

53. According to the professor what is key to the antimutagen process that can be found in the fire extinguishers?

54. What is the headline printed on the New York *Daily News* at the end of the film?

4

ARCHIE® COMIC BOOK SERIES: TMNT® ADVENTURES TRIVIA QUESTIONS

(Answers to Section Four begin on page 63.)

1. Who did Jess Harley become?
2. How did that happen?
3. Who is Mary Bones?
4. What was the crystal ball really?
5. What power does the Turnstone have?
6. Who is Stump?
7. Who is Stump's financial partner?
8. Who is Cudley?
9. What are his powers?
10. Who is Cryin' Houn'?

11. Where is Cryin' Houn' from?

12. Who is Ace Duck?

13. Where is Ace Duck from?

14. What Turtle wears a dark suit?

15. Why does he wear the dark suit?

16. Who is Scumbug?

17. Who is Wyrm?

18. What is the "Rat King's" name?

19. Who are the aliens who put the Turtles in a dream state?

20. What planet does Mary Bones take the Turtles to?

21. What color is the sun there?

22. What is Mary Bones's alien name?

23. Who does Krang summon to help defeat Cherubae and the Turtles?

24. What does he promise Maligna in return for her help?

25. What deal does Stump offer the Turtles for his help against Krang?

26. What wrestler joins the Turtles to help defeat Maligna's forces?

27. Where does Cherubae banish Krang to after his defeat?

28. Where does Cherubae send Shredder after his defeat?

29. What super animal being do the Turtles meet in Brazil?

30. What type of animal is Jagwar?

31. Where is Jagwar from?

32. What fruit does Jagwar give the Turtles as food to share in his vision?

33. Who seems to be behind the destruction of Jagwar's homeland?

34. What happens to April when she is in the rain forest?

35. Who is Paleocha?

36. What is a Tepui?

37. Who is Dreadmon?

38. What do the Coipacus call Dreadmon?

39. Who is Man Ray?

40. What is Man Ray's real name?

41. Who is Man Ray's sidekick?

42. What is Bubbla?

43. Who is Wingnut?

44. Where is Wingnut from?

45. Why has he vowed vengeance on Krang?

46. Who is Wingnut's sidekick?

47. What is Wingnut and Screwloose's relationship?

48. Who are Maligna's mutants that she sends to Earth?

49. Who do Scul and Bean make friends with on Earth?

50. What is Mr. Null's sea destruction plan called?

51. Who is Mondo Gecko?

52. What rock band did Mondo play with?

53. Who is Mondo Gecko's girlfriend?

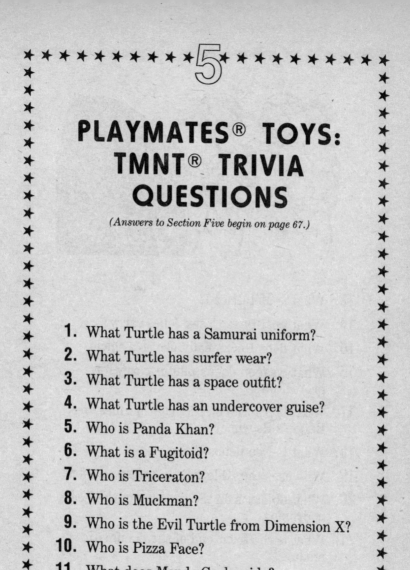

PLAYMATES® TOYS: TMNT® TRIVIA QUESTIONS

(Answers to Section Five begin on page 67.)

1. What Turtle has a Samurai uniform?
2. What Turtle has surfer wear?
3. What Turtle has a space outfit?
4. What Turtle has an undercover guise?
5. Who is Panda Khan?
6. What is a Fugitoid?
7. Who is Triceraton?
8. Who is Muckman?
9. Who is the Evil Turtle from Dimension X?
10. Who is Pizza Face?
11. What does Mondo Gecko ride?
12. What weapon does Scumbug carry?

13. What is MetalHead?

14. What gear does Casey Jones carry?

15. What does Rocksteady use as a shield?

16. What weapon does Splinter carry for protection?

17. What is printed on the flag that flies on Bebop's Psychocycle?

18. What is Needlenose?

19. Who uses the Killerbee as transportation?

20. What object is on the very top of the Technodrome?

21. What is the front end of the pneumatic module?

22. What powers Rocksteady's Footski?

23. What is the sidecar of the Turtle Cycle made out of?

24. What parts make up the Toilet Taxi?

25. What lethal substance is used in the Flush-o-Matic?

PART TWO

TRIVIA
QUESTION
ANSWERS

TMNT® CARTOON TRIVIA ANSWERS

A. Simple Level Answers:

1. Leonardo, Donatello, Michaelangelo, Raphael.
2. Four Renaissance artists.
3. Turtles fight with honor.
4. The Turtles' sensei (master teacher).
5. A rat.
6. In the sewers beneath New York City.
7. Pizza.
8. *Katana* (sword).
9. *Nunchaku.*
10. *Sai.*
11. *Bo.*
12. The Turtles' friend and ace newsreporter.
13. Channel 6.
14. A mini-video camera.

15. Burne.

16. Vernon.

17. April's secretary.

18. Shredder and Krang.

19. Rocksteady and Bebop.

20. Rocksteady is a rhino; Bebop is a warthog/boar.

21. The Foot Clan.

22. Foot Soldiers.

23. Robots.

24. A footprint.

25. Death stars.

26. An evil brain from outerspace.

27. In a giant android body.
28. Dimension X.
29. Portal openings.
30. The Technodrome.
31. Buried in the center of the Earth.
32. Pneumatic module transporter.
33. A villainous general from Dimension X.
34. Rock Soldiers.
35. Turtle communicator.
36. A small turtle shell.
37. The Turtle van.
38. The Turtle blimp.
39. The Turtle glider.
40. A motorized skateboard the Turtles use in the sewers.
41. Cowabunga, dude.

B. Medium Level Answers:

42. Ninjutsu.
43. Shredhead.
44. Shellbacks.
45. Leatherhead.
46. By 'Gar; I Gar'ntee.
47. A vigilante who fights crime in the city.
48. A hockey stick.
49. A ghoulish man who lives in the city and controls the rats.
50. Mutant frogs/teenagers similar in origin to the Turtles.
51. The Okefenokee Swamp in Florida.

52. Trenchcoats, hats, and human face masks.

53. Leonardo.

54. Donatello.

55. The Fly.

56. Shredder's mad scientist.

57. A robot built to destroy the Turtles.

58. A police robot built to protect the city.

59. A mechanical spider built by Baxter Stockman.

60. A robot that looks like Irma.

61. It could destroy anything that looked like a turtle, or whatever it thought was a turtle.

C. "Stumpers" Answers:

62. Lotus.

63. A lotus blossom flower.

64. Oroku Saki.

65. Hamato Yoshi.

66. Hannah Avenue.

67. A giant globe of the world.

68. Princess Mallory.

69. Joe's Pizza.

70. Pizza delivery boy.

71. A catwoman.

72. Tiffany.

73. "Happy Hour News."

74. Attila, Napoleon, Genghis, Rasputin.

75. Attila, Napoleon, and Genghis were world conquerors; Rasputin a royal court official.

76. Bullwhip, Bow/Arrow, Mace, and Battle-ax.

77. The Nutrinos.

78. Zak, Dax, and Kala.

D. Specific Episode Answers:

79. Michaelangelo.

80. A flying hot rod (sports car).

81. A fluffy pet/monster from Dimension X.

82. Kala, the Nutrino.

83. Psychic Kinetic Energy: the ability to move objects with thought.

84. He becomes a monster.

85. Soak him in water.

86. Usagi Yojimbo.

87. He is a master Samurai warrior.

88. Aunt Aggie.

89. Big Red.

90. The Great Boldini.

91. Zach.

92. He found Raphael's Turtlecom.

93. He plugs his microphone feed into the Turtlecom to produce feedback.

94. One hundred pounds of gold.

95. Leonardo.

96. So that she will report on the virtues of rats as pets.

97. With a pied pipe.

98. To control Splinter with his pipe, so that the Ninja Master will teach his rats the skills to take over the city.

99. An evil computer programmed to destroy the Turtles.

100. A magical alien elf from Dimension X.

101. REX-1.

102. Robot Enforcement Experiment #1.

103. An alien crystal converger.

104. A household plant.

105. Omnus.

106. Puts it on his helmet, to tap into his mental powers.

107. Channel 6's van driver, Blodget; then Baxter Stockman.

108. Doku plant.

109. Gazi leaf.

110. Polarity Deflector.

111. Niagara Falls Power Plant.

112. Mutant creature eggs accidentally planted on pizza.

113. In the microwave oven.

114. Mighty Rocksteady and Super Bebop.

115. "Trial."

116. Gravity boots.

117. A hamster.

118. Octopuss Inc.

119. Casey Jones.

120. They lead it into a fun house mirror room, where it malfunctions trying to destroy all the mirror Turtle images.

121. The Punk Frogs.

122. He leads them into quicksand.

123. He rejuvenates into a child.

124. Michaelangelo.
125. A napkin.
126. Four hundred years.
127. The Docilator.

TMNT® MOVIE TRIVIA ANSWERS

A. Simple Level Answers:

1. New York City.
2. April O'Neil.
3. Channel 3.
4. Charles Pennington.
5. Danny.
6. Foot Clan.
7. Raphael.
8. A *sai*.
9. Dominoes.
10. Raphael.
11. Michaelangelo.
12. Raphael.

April works for Channel 3.

13. He rescues her from a second encounter with the Foot Clan.

14. Casey Jones.

15. A hockey mask.

16. A hockey stick.

17. Antiques.

18. Splinter.

19. Raphael.

20. It is destroyed and set afire during a fight.

21. A country home belonging to an unspecified relative.

22. Danny.

23. Casey Jones.

24. He dresses in a Foot Soldier uniform.

25. Shredder killed Splinter's master and his master's girlfriend.

26. He clawed Shredder's face permanently.

27. He sliced a bit off of Splinter's ear.

28. Splinter battles him, and Shredder falls off a rooftop.

29. In a garbage truck.

30. WTRL.

31. 2nd Time Around—Antiques & more.

32. April's dad.

33. Raphael.

34. Twenty dollars.

35. "Boss-a-nova."

36. Anchovies.

37. Invisibility.

38. *Critters.*

39. Cricket.

40. A professional hockey player.

41. Donatello.

42. Battle axes.

43. A golf club.

44. Honor.

45. In the cartoon: Splinter was Yoshi, who mutated into a rat. In the movie: Splinter was Master Yoshi's pet rat.

46. Sid.

47. Sid Vicious, member of the English punk band, "The Sex Pistols."

48. "City Crime Escalates."

49. "The Silent Crime Wave."

50. Sterns.

51. Mario's Diaper Service.

52. Shadows.

53. "Tequilla."

54. Two minutes.

55. To LaGuardia Airport.

56. A Jose Consuella.

57. 11th Street and Bleecker.

58. A panda bear.

59. Little ducks with umbrellas.

60. "It's Worse—NY Crime on the Rise."

61. City Hall.

62. Master Tatsu.

63. A driver.

64. A dragon *dogi*.

65. The story of the Tortoise and the Hare.

66. Donatello.

67. *Gilligan's Island.*

68. Donatello.

69. Trivial Pursuit.

70. Claustrophobia; fear of enclosure.

71. Tang Shen.

72. Leonardo.

73. A pike.

74. The East Warehouse on Landman Island.

75. Donatello.

TMNT® II: THE SECRET OF THE OOZE™ MOVIE TRIVIA ANSWERS

A. Simple Level Answers:

1. Pizza.
2. Keno.
3. In a garbage can.
4. Michaelangelo.
5. Sausages.
6. April's apartment.
7. Back flips.
8. T.G.R.I.
9. In New Jersey.
10. Dandelions.
11. A wolf and a snapping turtle.

12. In an abandoned subway station.

13. Vanilla Ice.

14. He is blown away by the sound speakers when Michaelangelo plays the guitar.

15. He mutates into "SuperShredder."

16. The dock falls apart and crushes him.

B. Medium Level Answers:

17. Roy's pizza.

18. A toy store, electronics store, pizza stand.

19. "Walk the Dog" and "Around the World."

20. A rubber snake.

21. The Foot Clan.

22. Raphael.

23. With a giant net.

24. A bow and arrow.

25. Tokka.

26. Rahzar.

27. Ice cubes.

28. Doughnuts.

29. A fire extinguisher.

30. "Ninja Rap."

Splinter shoots down the net with a bow and arrow.

31. Keno.

32. They are turtles so they swim and then float to the surface of the water.

C. "Stumpers" Answers:

33. 11th Street and Sixth Avenue.

34. Spring Street and Lower Broadway.

35. Raphael.

36. Technoglobal Research Industries.

37. Professor Jordon Perry.

38. Freddy.

39. R-708-037.

40. Paulina Porizkova.

41. *Casablanca*.

42. Phil.

43. "Swimsuits in the 90's."

44. Fifteen.

45. The Brooklyn Bridge.

46. Mama.

47. News Van Eight.

48. Precinct Fourteen.

49. 338 Kelvin.

50. A Bart Simpson drinking glass.

51. Dockside Club.

52. The mutants burp, which retards the process.

53. Carbon dioxide.

54. "Ninja Rap Is Born."

4

ARCHIE® COMIC BOOK SERIES: TMNT® ADVENTURES TRIVIA ANSWERS

1. "Leatherhead."

2. Mary Bones turned him into it for stealing her crystal ball.

3. A swamp witch, banished from Dimension X.

4. The Turnstone.

5. It is a directional thought transanimator.

6. A tree mutant and intergalactic wrestling promoter.

7. Sling.

8. A Transdimensional Cowlick.

9. Transporting beings from dimensions through his mouth.

10. A four-armed mutant scourge and intergalactic wrestler.

11. The Bohunkian Galaxy.

12. An intergalactic wrestler on the Stump network.

13. The Planet Perdufus.

14. Raphael.

15. He chose to wear it to exert his individuality.

16. A human who worked as an exterminator who was bathed in mutagen, transforming him into a giant Cockroach Man.

17. A mutant planarian worm that lives in the sewers.

18. Ha'ntaan.

19. The Sons of Silence.

20. Hirobyl.

21. Red.

22. Cherubae.

23. Maligna.

24. To devour Earth's resources.

25. His wrestlers' help in exchange for television broadcast rights.

26. Trap.

27. Morbus, the toxic waste dump world.

28. To a prison on Earth.

29. Jagwar.

30. A jaguar mutant.

31. The rain forest.

32. Jangala.

33. Mr. Null.

34. Mr. Null's men kidnap her.

35. Woman leader of the Coipacu tribe that lives in the rain forest.

36. The Coipacu's home: sandstone mesas in the hills.

37. A werewolf-type creature that lives in the rain forest.

38. Lobo.

39. A mutant manta ray.

40. Ray Fillet.

41. Bubbla.

42. A mutant fish creature.

43. A crazed mutant batlike creature.

44. The Planet Huanu.

45. Krang attacked and destroyed Wingnut's planet.

46. Screwloose.

47. Screwloose feeds on Wingnut, his sting allows the bat to sleep.

48. Scul and Bean.

49. Mr. Null.

50. "Deep Dump Operation."

51. A teenage boy mutated with a gecko.

52. "Merciless Slaughter."

53. Candace.

PLAYMATES® TOYS: TMNT® TRIVIA ANSWERS

1. Leonardo.

2. Michaelangelo.

3. Raphael.

4. Donatello.

5. A Samurai panda bear.

6. A robot.

7. A mutant triceratops (dinosaur).

8. A mutant garbage ghoul.

9. Slash.

10. A mutant psychotic pizza chef.

11. A skateboard.

12. An insect exterminator gun.

13. A robot in the form of a Turtle.

14. A hockey stick and a broken baseball bat.

15. A sewer drain cover.

16. A bow and arrow.

17. "Sleezy Rider."

18. A mutant mosquito crossed with a jet fighter.

19. The Foot Soldiers.

20. A giant eyeball viewer.

21. A powerful earth drill.

22. Electrical leeches.

23. A garbage can.

24. A toilet and a shower.

25. Ooze.

CELEBRATING
YEARLING
25 YEARS

Yearling Books
celebrates its
25 years—
and salutes
Reading Is
Fundamental®
on its 25th
anniversary.

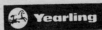